IMAGES
of America

RUMSON

With best wishes to Doug
Send those old Rumson pics starting
for Volume II
Randall Gabrielan
September 21, 1996
Rumson

IMAGES
of America

RUMSON

Randall Gabrielan

ARCADIA

ISBN 0-7524-0290-0

Published by Arcadia Publishing,
an imprint of the Chalford Publishing Corporation
One Washington Center, Dover, New Hampshire 03820
Printed in Great Britain

*I am pleased to dedicate this book to my good friend George H. Moss Jr.,
who will forever be linked to Rumson and history.
The public knows him as the author
of Monmouth County's finest historical works of his half of this century.
Those close to him revere him as an affectionate family man,
a loyal public servant,
and a warm, helpful historical companion and colleague.*

Contents

Acknowledgments

The author is grateful for the friendship and dedication to history of John Rhody, Robert Schoeffling, and Michael Steinhorn—three collectors whose holdings are open before a project starts. He is pleased to present images from the Moss Archives, a source most often seen in the stellar publications of George Moss. Thanks to Joseph Carney for making available W.J. Leonard's *Sea Bright Rumson Road Oceanic Monmouth Beach Atlantic Highlands Leonardville Road Navesink Water Witch Club* (Sea Bright: The Sentinel, 1903), an important work deserving wider recognition (it is hereafter referred to in the text as *Seaside Souvenir*, to save space). The author expresses his thanks, appreciation, and esteem to Edith Borden and Suzanne Parmly, who shared not only their pictures, but their family histories, two of the most important to Rumson. With special thanks to Photography Unlimited by Dorn's, and to Kathy Dorn Severini for uncovering their outstanding contributions to this volume. Dorn's has long been acclaimed as the photographic archive of Red Bank. An on-going cataloguing of their negatives is revealing treasures that will give them similar stature for the entire region surrounding Red Bank.

Thanks to all who, with contributions of single or many images, became the co-producers of this volume: Olga Boeckel; Richard F. Doughty; Marti Huber; Gail Hunton; W. Edmund Kemble; Noboru Kobayashi; the Honorable Theodore J. Labrecque; Evelyn Leavens; John Lentz; Ann Marie Lynch; Mr. and Mrs. Q.A. Shaw McKean Jr.; Timothy J. McMahon; the Monmouth County Historical Association; Thomas and Elizabeth O'Mara; the Red Bank Public Library; Special Collections and Archives, Rutgers University Libraries; Karen L. Schnitzspahn; Frances Statter; Marjorie Tedesco; Roberta Van Anda; Mary Weir; Keith Wells; Lawrence E. White; and Marilyn Willis.

Rumson Place Names

Familiarity with Rumson's place names is a helpful aid to understanding its history. Early Native American expressions, including "Navarumsunk" and a simpler version, "Narrumson" (which is still preserved as a street name), evolved into today's Rumson. Variations of Rumson were first used in the 1660s, but the borough was not formed from Shrewsbury Township until 1907. Numerous locality names arose in the years between. Their use often overlapped and there was generally no linear progression. Some of them still survive as neighborhoods.

One of the first sites of Rumson settlement was Black Point. Early written references to the settlement date as early as 1736, and the area was mapped by 1765. Located on the Navesink River, Black Point benefited greatly from its proximity to one of the inlets that pierced the barrier beach at Sandy Hook, providing ready access to the sea. The settlement's importance can be inferred from its status as a destination on the road from Shrewsbury—the earliest settlement on the mainland south of Rumson. The major section of the Shrewsbury-Black Point Road is now Rumson Road. Black Point is also remembered in a street name, Black Point Horseshoe. The settlement's most important building is pictured on p. 104.

The two river shores of Rumson rise to a range of hills once known collectively as the Rumson Hills. Ridge Road runs along their crest. Rumson Hills was used as the locality for the area's most prominent estate, "Rohallion," although the name applies to a broad stretch of land rather than a specific spot.

Sea Bright was coined with the 1870 development of the ocean shore area that is now the center of the borough of Sea Bright, which was formed from Ocean Township in 1889. Sea Bright was spelled as one word for some years (as in the Seabright Lawn Tennis and Cricket Club), and was applied to much of eastern Rumson, with usage apparently at least as far west as an estate on Bellevue Avenue.

The Rumson shore of the Shrewsbury River, the first to be developed after the 1870 opening of the Sea Bright Bridge, was known early on as Rumson Bluff. However, this apparent effort to distinguish it from the barrier beach shore did not stem the widespread use of Sea Bright throughout eastern Rumson. The name Rumson Beach was given to a stretch of shore in Sea Bright opposite Rumson, an apparent reciprocal gesture of confusion.

Little Silver, on Rumson's western border, was formed from Shrewsbury Township in 1923. It, too, has been applied to Rumson locales and residents. Press references to Rumson people and events are often found in neighboring towns' news columns, and one such Little Silver reference was noted as far east as Buena Vista Avenue.

Village life in Rumson developed at Port Washington, spurred by Thomas Hunt's *c.* 1840 purchase of investment property near today's Oceanic Bridge. The village probably owes its name to the proximity of its development to the 1832 George Washington centennial, celebrated in honor of the founding father, whose name appears in places and streets more than any other person. A village in those days was often little more than a place of public gathering, generally consisting of a store, church or mill, and a few houses. The name Port Washington remained in use until 1871, when a post office was established. Federal authorities required that the name be changed to avoid confusion with the existing office at Port Washington, New York, and as a result the name Oceanic was coined.

Oceanic, containing the core of Rumson's year-round population, was long the focus of community life. Most of Rumson's spiritual, social, and community organizations began there, including the Village Improvement Society. The campaign to establish Rumson as a borough was led by Oceanic's permanent residents.

A second, early, year-round settlement arose west of Black Point and east of Oceanic. Established by the 1890s, it was founded substantially by watermen and workers on the nearby estates, and is still known today as East Oceanic.

Cartonville was in use by the 1880s, apparently consisting of a small group residing around the Cartons rather than an extensive neighborhood. The importance of trolley travel early in this century and the prominence of stores in the creation of local names gave rise to Hintelmanns Corner, a name that lasted longer than the streetcars.

The name Rumson appears in at least two other place names: Rumson Waterway and Rumson Park. The former is a man-made navigable widening of Ivins Creek, an improvement made to enhance the value of the surrounding land. The latter is a neighborhood developed concurrently with the Rumson Country Club; its name is prominent on an entrance sign, if not in regular usage.

Three real estate investment colonies were established in the Rumson Road area in 1882, one to the north, one on its western stem, and one near the Shrewsbury River. The first two, Belbea (or Belknap) Park and Ellesmere Park respectively, were small, well-designed and landscaped communities, whose names have been forgotten. The third, established by William W. Conover, changed its name after he divested from Conover Park to West Park. Its character has also changed, with the recent intensive development of costly houses.

The numerous islands off Rumson merit a separate study. The most-widely known and inhabited, Barley Point Island, has the same name as its owner-corporation, although it has not been ascertained which was named first. A second, Msgr. Kelley Island, has been given the imprimatur of a borough resolution. The list is not complete, but covers the potential for confusion.

References

For those interested in further investigating the history of the area, the author suggests the following:

The Rumson Historical Commitee's *History of Rumson 1665–1944* (Asbury Park, NJ: 1944.)

W.J. Leonard's *Sea Bright Rumson Road Oceanic Monmouth Beach Atlantic Highlands Leonardville Road Navesink Water Witch Club* (Sea Bright: The Sentinel, 1903.)

George H. Moss Jr.'s *Nauvoo to the Hook* (Sea Bright: NJ, 1964) and *Another Look at Nauvoo to the Hook* (Sea Bright: NJ, 1990.)

Randall Gabrielan's Rumson enties in "Great Homes," a monthly column in *The Two River Times*.

One

Sea Bright Bridge and Rumson Bluff

The *Wilber A. Heisley*, a 185-foot steamer built in 1883 at Nyack, New York, was the only stern-wheeler on local waters. Its career was short, as its design did not facilitate turning and it tended to run aground. It was renamed the *City of Long Branch* in 1885. The boat was sold *c.* 1889; it was destroyed by fire in 1892. The vessel is shown here in 1885 against the background of the Rumson Bluff—Ward Avenue today—with the house above the wheel shown on p. 19.

Linking Rumson to the shore at Sea Bright by a bridge provided not only a span of transport, but the foundation for the building of the former town. The bridge was built in 1870 by ten organizers of the private Jumping Point Drawbridge Company. Their initiative was prompted by their land holdings, which were enhanced in value with the new link to the shore. The tollhouse was moved to a Sea Bright site, and is still used as a residence. It is shown here in a c. 1900 photograph.

This 1901 image provides a view of a temporary bridge, the third, that was built south of Rumson Road, connecting with Sea Bright's Peninsula Avenue. The Sea Bright Bridge was purchased by the county c. 1888. A major struggle over fair compensation for the owners took years to settle.

A number of young people emerge from an opening span of the fourth Sea Bright Bridge around the late 1940s. Safety standards of the day permitted travelers to stay on an opening draw and even jump off the moving span. The view is east, toward Sea Bright. The Sea Bright Beach Club is at left, with the former Sea Bright Inn at right. The latter had a deck over the water. (The Dorn's Collection.)

A small child seems even more diminutive dwarfed by three-story houses on one of Rumson's finest residential streets. Ward Avenue has changed a great deal since this c. 1910 photograph was taken. (Collection of John Rhody.)

Rumson Road's curve north at Ward Avenue is so frequently encountered that one readily forgets the road ran straight across the river. The site of the Neeser-Barbour house (see p. 14), which had been demolished some years earlier, became the new bridge approach, seen here as construction was nearing completion in early 1951. The body of water at top left is Oyster Bay. Perhaps the most noteworthy difference forty-five years ago was the lack of development in

West Park around the bay. The area around Saint George's Church, at left near the shore, can be compared with the aerial view on p. 121. The Sea Bright Beach Club is in the left foreground. The windmill on p. 15 is visible at right center. Note Holy Cross's former rectory, adjacent to the church at right. (The Dorn's Collection.)

J.C. Neeser of New York had this house built on the northeast corner of Rumson Road and Ward Avenue by local contractor Charles L. Walters in 1890–91, architect unknown. It was bought in 1918 by Mrs. William Barbour, after she sold her Rumson Road property (p. 43). The house was demolished for expected development of the lot, but the property became the road approach to the 1951 Sea Bright Bridge. This is a *c.* 1910 postcard. (Collection of Michael Steinhorn.)

The house at 9 North Ward Avenue was built in 1870 by William W. Shippen, a civil engineer, a real estate developer, and a partner in the development of Sea Bright. His house originally stood in Sea Bright on the beach near the Sea Bright Bridge and railroad station. It was damaged in the storms of 1913 and 1914 and moved by barge to its present location. It was originally clapboard-covered, with Stick Style ornamentation and shingle cladding added later. (From the *Monmouth Pictorial*, Autumn 1939.)

The octagonal windmill structure at 37 Ward Avenue is one of the last two left in Rumson, a town once dotted with them by the scores. The windmill was erected around 1895 by the A.J. Corcoran Company of Jersey City. Andrew J. Corcoran was an Irish immigrant who perfected the mechanical devices of the windmill pump and manufactured windmills from his own patented designs.

Anyone familiar with the Ward Avenue streetscape must be curious about the interior of the windmill, so here it is. Corcoran's promotional material claimed that he had two hundred windmills over a 5-mile stretch of Rumson Road.

The Church of the Holy Cross was built on the west side of Ward Avenue in 1885 and dedicated the next year. The shingle-clad, Gothic Revival edifice was designed by P.C. Kelly and built by John Burke of Asbury Park. A rectory was added south of the church. The once narrow lot was expanded over the years; church property now includes a 600-foot frontage on the north side of Rumson Road for Holy Cross School.

The church's original altar was replaced in 1948 and donated to Saint Catherine's Church in Middletown Township. This altar was installed then and modified in 1969 to facilitate worship changes directed by the Second Vatican Council.

H.T. Hadden built this house in 1889 on the north side of Rumson Road, east of the Seabright Lawn Tennis and Cricket Club. It was designed by Sidney Stratton, who used a blank contract from his former architectural firm of McKim, Mead, and White to write up the agreement with the Haddens! The building featured elements of the emerging Colonial Revival style. It is no longer extant; the site is now occupied by Holy Cross School. (From *Seaside Souvenir*.)

Samuel J. Harriot built this Colonial Revival house, designed by Sidney Stratton, at the northwest corner of Rumson Road and Ward Avenue. The house was later owned by New York broker Bernon S. Prentice, a key figure at the Seabright Lawn Tennis and Cricket Club who was largely responsible for the club's prominence on the touring circuit. The house was infrequently used after Prentice left; it was sold to Holy Cross Church c. 1940, and was demolished in 1963 after being replaced by a modern facility. It is shown here c. 1910. (The Moss Archives.)

The view north from the corner of Rumson Road and Ward Avenue shows the Harriot/Prentice house (p. 17) and Holy Cross (p. 16) in the context of their landscape. The old rectory is not visible, but the house's garage still stands and is used by the church for storage. At top are the Navesink River and the Hartshorne Woods hills (at right). The picture is likely *c.* 1920.

Malcolm Graham's carriage house at 31 Ward Avenue was designed by H. Edwards Ficken of New York in the Shingle Style and built in 1885. The integrity of the structure has been preserved and it retains the atmosphere of its early days. The tower on the east is decorative. Renovations for residential occupancy include the installation of a porch from the former Holy Cross convent on the north as well as living room floor boards taken from an Ocean Grove church. Horse stalls have even been incorporated into living space.

Robert Belknap was likely the original owner of this house on 17 North Ward Avenue that was built c. 1870. It was later owned by John V. Fraley, who, according to W.J. Leonard, "improved the property to a choice bluff residence." Alfred N. Beadleston, the father of the long-time state senator and a brewer, bought the house in 1897. Its Stick Style beginnings will surprise many who are familiar with the current facade of this prominent riverfront house. It is shown here c. 1890s. (The Moss Archives.)

The house was extensively remodeled in the Colonial Revival style, although it is not clear when. The noted radio figure Major Bowes bought the place—then named "Riveredge"—in 1938. He broadcast many of his "Amateur Hour" programs from here. Bowes died in 1946, leaving the house to the Catholic church in New York. This view was published in the late 1930s in the *Monmouth Pictorial*. There have been later alterations, but this east facade is recognizable today.

Charles and Mary Ward bought 40 acres of the Parmly estate in 1869, anticipating the construction of the Sea Bright Bridge. They subdivided their property, leaving their name on the street. Charles A. Peabody built the origins of this Shingle Style house on the Shrewsbury River, architect unknown. The Peabodys stayed only a few years, selling to Thomas and Harriet Carmichael in 1898. This view of the west facade is from *Seaside Souvenir*.

The Carmichaels remodeled, giving the house its present appearance. Their architects were Rossiter and Wright, New Yorkers with an active shore practice (see p. 29). The house, shown here in a c. 1910 postcard view, is one of two in Rumson designated as "The Lindens." The land attached to this property long included an uninhabited island, which was donated to the Borough of Rumson in 1993 by owner Monsignor James Francis Kelley. The island is now named for him. (Collection of Michael Steinhorn.)

Two
Rumson Road

The Seabright Lawn Tennis and Cricket Club on Rumson Road and Tennis Court Lane was founded in 1877 and is the oldest continuously active tennis club in the United States. It was for many years an important site on the eastern tennis circuit, the club's Seabright Invitational Tournament attracting most major players until mid-century. The Shingle Style clubhouse with Tudor Revival elements was built in 1886 and designed by noted New York architects Renwick, Aspinwall, and Russell. Altered on several occasions, the building is seen here looking north from Rumson Road. The clubhouse was designated a National Historic Landmark in 1992. (From *Seaside Souvenir*.)

James M. Allgor's desire to establish a business at the foot of Rumson Road—a celebrated drive of country estates—pre-dated zoning and land regulation. However, Allgor clashed with the rules of order that prevailed. He protested the exertions of several community leaders eager to preserve standards, by hanging women's undergarments emblazoned with the names of his adversaries on a clothesline at the opening of Saint George's Church. This Dorn's Collection photograph of unknown provenance appears to portray that event. The garments were taken down by local officials and used as evidence in legal proceedings against him.

James M. Allgor's origins and death have eluded the author, but it is known he was a carpenter in Sea Bright at the end of the nineteenth century. He announced his intention to open an ice cream store and confectionery at the foot of Rumson Road, on a lot that was partially vacant. His shop is visible behind one of his many protest messages on what were known as spite fences. The building is now a private residence at 1 Rumson Road. (Collection of John Rhody.)

Nearly all of the Allgor spite fence views are from photographic postcards that Allgor made and sold for income. Establishing their dates is problematic. This one appears to be 1911–12, when Wilson was governor, perhaps during a spell when Allgor was imprisoned. Rumson passed an ordinance in 1910 banning unlicensed signboards. (Collection of John Rhody.)

Allgor was not the best speller. His messages are often semi-coherent, but one wonders what measure of truth is in his allegations. Was a Rumson Road gentleman a smuggler? (Collection of John Rhody.)

Each line is painted on individual boards, which were nailed to posts such as those visible above. At times the progress of the signs can be traced through their changes. Note the names of his adversaries on this one, which are painted out below. If there is one easily remembered pithy crack amongst his rantings, it may be, "The poor who steal go to prison, while the rich go to Europe." (Collection of the Red Bank Public Library.)

Regulations regarding the heights of signs constituted another effort to control Allgor. Note his assertion, "All poor men should be socialist." Allgor was a member of Red Bank's socialist organization, but many members denounced his activities, feeling he should not invoke their cause in settling a personal dispute. Note his gun mounted on the sign. Allgor was given a six-month prison term in 1913 for accosting Charles Halsey in the street. (Collection of John Rhody.)

One wonders what shipbuilding trust and watered stock case, if any, is referenced. This is a rare instance of a pictorial fence. It's not really a bad painting. (Collection of John Rhody.)

Allgor's fences wrapped around three sides of his property. This one shows the east as well as the north side, which faced the street. A fence on the west side is at the bottom of p. 23. Note the reference to "insane asylum," where Allgor was taken at least twice. The property was sold in a sheriff's sale in 1914. Allgor owned a houseboat. The author's last trace of him is a news account of a contest over an asylum commission in 1915. (Collection of John Rhody.)

The house at 3 Rumson Road was labeled "Fort Packer" in the July 1911 *American Suburbs Monmouth County Edition*, where builder Peter Benson had it illustrated over his business description entry. The original owner, P. Hall Packer, was an early mayor of Sea Bright. The cladding gives a basic four-square house a Romanesque Revival look and the inspiration for the name "fort." The present owner, artist Barbara Cocker, indicated that the surface is cast Swedish hollow concrete block. The large air space behind the walls provides natural insulation.

George F. Vietor, senior partner of New York dry goods importer Vietor and Achelis, built this massive Shingle Style house in 1893 on the south side of Rumson Road, opposite the tennis club. The architects were the New York firm of Lamb and Rich, who had an active shore practice. Vietor died in 1910, his widow Annie surviving him by seventeen years. They were the parents of Thomas, who built the house on p. 36. Modern houses are on the George Vietor site now. (From *Seaside Souvenir*.)

Named houses fascinate, but one wonders how this Shingle Style Colonial Revival example at the eastern stem of Rumson Road became known as "Mona Lisa." Its origins are not clear (possibly it was moved to a once-narrow lot by R.D. White). It was Henry Soulier's residence at the time this *c.* 1910 postcard was published. His estate sold the house in 1941. (Collection of John Rhody.)

Robert Lenox Belknap developed Belbea Park north of Rumson Road around today's Belknap Lane in 1882. He was a founder of Columbia's chapter of Phi Beta Kappa, active in the New York National Guard, and an official of the railroad. Belknap had a residence on Rumson Bluff. Belbea Park, which the reliable W.J. Leonard also referred to as Belknap Park, appears to have been a planned investment community. This house, shown here *c.* 1890s, was identified as "No. 1" on a large-scale water system map of 1883; it may have been Belknap's own house. It stands today as 3 Belknap Lane, its appearance obscured by alterations and a recent large addition.

Bruce Price designed this house at 55 Rumson Road for Dr. Charles R. Shepard of New York, who sold it in unfinished condition to Theodore Moss, for whom the house is historically named. It was built in 1889 by local contractor J.E. Denise, and is shown here in a *c.* 1910 postcard view. Its decorative restraint makes it a fine example of early Colonial Revival architecture in Rumson.

The most visible changes to 55 Rumson Road have been the building-up of the west wing to two-and-one-half stories and the addition of gabled dormers on the sides of the original one in the center. The ivy on the older picture obscures detail, but this recent picture reveals a partial brick wall that extends from the foundation to the top of the first floor. Note that the eastern end has also been built up with a roof line continuous with the original main block.

The south elevation of 55 Rumson Road appears to double as a second front entrance. It probably saw greater utility when the property, since divided, continued to South Shrewsbury Drive. Shown here c. 1910, a garage now stands in the left foreground and a redesigned porch is now enclosed.

The Marie Stuart Palmer house at 54 Rumson Road was built in 1894. It was designed by architects Rossiter and Wright and constructed by local builders Pearsall and Bogle. Ehrick Rossiter was a nephew of Ehrick Parmly of Bingham Hill, and Frank A. Wright was an officer of the Water Witch Club, predecessor of today's Monmouth Hills. The house is a fine, well-preserved early Colonial Revival. Modifications have been minor, including the removal of the second-story balustrades, and the house's integrity is intact. This is a c. 1905 postcard. (Collection of Michael Steinhorn.)

Who is the only member of baseball's Hall of Fame to have owned a Rumson country house? Albert Goodwill Spalding was an outstanding pitcher early in his career for Chicago, pitching shutouts in his first two starts and winning an incredible forty-six games in 1876, while managing his team. He bought William Everhard Strong's estate at the northwest corner of Rumson Road and the Avenue of Two Rivers in 1893. Spalding stayed only eight years; this 1899 view was taken late in his ownership.

David Lamar, a securities speculator who tangled with big-time adversaries (including J.P. Morgan) to earn the nefarious nickname of "The Wolf of Wall Street," bought the estate in 1901. He defaulted and Spalding sued. A high-powered legal struggle followed. The case was decided in Spalding's favor in the U.S. Supreme Court, his interest represented by leading Red Bank lawyer Edmund Wilson. The carriage house is the only estate building remaining with its integrity intact. It was converted to a private residence and is home to the family of Michael Steinhorn, C.P.A., history enthusiast, helpful supporter of the author, and owner of this picture.

James R. Williston, a New York broker, bought the place in 1907. Watson and Huckel of Philadelphia executed major remodeling in the Colonial Revival style in 1915, giving the house this appearance. This view was published in various *Monmouth Pictorials* in the late 1930s. Williston jumped to his death in 1931. Three years later, the broke and defeated Lamar died, obscure and alone in a New York hotel room. Mrs. Williston's attempts to sell in a poor depression market were unsuccessful. The house was destroyed by fire in 1938.

Howard S. Borden's business interests included Rumson house building. He bought the Williston tract *c.* 1941, naming his proposed real estate development Pine Ridge. This *c.* 1940s postcard shows the property's outlines: Rumson Road is at right and Ridge Road is at left, with the eastern boundary, the Avenue of Two Rivers, connecting the two in the center of the photograph. His Old Farm Village in the Oceanic area was an acclaimed success, and he aimed to replicate that orderly neighborhood of well-designed buildings in Pine Ridge. (Collection of Michael Steinhorn.)

House construction at Pine Ridge began around November 1, 1941. Timing was not favorable, with the war and resultant materials shortages only a month away. Frank W. Cole, architect of Asbury Park, was hired for architectural supervision of the property, although it is not known if he designed this early house. This Colonial Revival built at the northwest corner of the Avenue of Two Rivers and Clover Lane still stands, its appearance unaltered. It is shown here in a 1940s postcard. (Collection of Michael Steinhorn.)

This 1940s postcard shows the Pine Ridge real estate office at the northwest corner of the Avenue of Two Rivers and Blossom Lane. It is well preserved and still a real estate office, now occupied by Gloria Woodward Associates. (Collection of Michael Steinhorn.)

Arthur B. Jennings, a New York architect better known for his church and educational work, designed this house for Joseph T. Low at the northeast corner of Rumson Road and the Avenue of Two Rivers. Low, a native of Louisville, Kentucky, was in the dry goods business in New York. L.S. Wolff owned the house by 1897, when it was reported that he was enlarging it. Wolff also maintained ownership when this postcard was published c. 1910. The house no longer stands. (Collection of John Rhody.)

The oldest section of the house at 86 Rumson Road was built in 1879 for Thomas de Sotolongo, an apparent employee of his Rumson Road neighbor, Jose F. de Navarro. It was designed by Boston native Edward H. Kendall, whose architectural firm was in New York. This view is the south facade, showing part of the major 1898 expansion made by then owner W.A. Bloodgood. The house once had the nickname "Fairyleigh."

Johnfritz and Louise Achelis bought the property at 60 Rumson Road in 1924 and commissioned New York architects Hyde and Shepherd to design this Tudor Revival house. It was probably built shortly afterward. The house first received wide notice with a six-page pictorial review in the October 1929 issue of *The Architect*. Achelis, using the family business for acquisitions, became active in factoring, eventually heading the Commercial Factors Division of CIT Financial Corporation. This view is the south elevation facing the street, seen in its present state.

The north facade of 60 Rumson Road presents an interesting design oddity—the side away from public view has the more decorative detailing, with its Tudor design elements readily apparent, particularly the steep roof. This example of the more artfully designed facade facing away from the street is contrary to the usual practice in Rumson.

The William A. Street house, known as "The Hermitage," stands at 79 Rumson Road at its southwest corner with the Avenue of Two Rivers. This Shingle Style masterpiece, designed by New York's McKim, Mead, and White, was built in 1883 and is the only example of that firm's work in the area with intact integrity. Two earlier driveways are no longer in use; a driveway added later now leads to the west side of the house. A garage, designed by architect George Rudolph and constructed in the late-1980s, has the character of both carriage house and gate house, providing a compatible enhancement to the house.

Harden L. Crawford, a son of Robert Leighton Crawford (see p. 40) and summer resident of Atlantic Highlands, built the house at 89 Rumson Road in 1903. When *The Sentinel* reported, "It will not be built by contract. The architect Mr. Lowell will have charge," it left historians wondering which Lowell designed this handsome house embracing varied motifs of the time.

The house Harrie T. Lindeberg designed for Thomas F. Vietor at 99 Rumson Road is arguably Rumson's most artistic twentieth-century landmark. Lindeberg specialized in country houses, with the English Tudor Revival being one of his preferred styles. The still large house was once massive, with its wing on the east removed in 1952, that part forming the basic blocks of two additional houses built on the west side of Bingham Avenue. A one-story garage was added to that end, visible at left.

The living room contains this nearly 7-foot-tall marble fireplace. Lindeberg preferred fireplaces to rise higher, rather than wider. The barely discernable metalwork presents a bird motif, one followed in architectural decoration throughout the house. The room has been likened to a concert hall and fittingly contains two pianos and an organ. This picture is courtesy of Lloyd Christainson, who has occupied the house for nearly half of its seventy-eight years. The place deserves to be called The Christainson House, in honor of Lloyd and his late beloved wife Sergie.

The property attached to 99 Rumson Road once extended to the Shrewsbury River. It was subdivided and Pompano Road opened behind the Vietor outbuildings. The former superintendent's residence, which fronts on the north side of that street, is shown here in a c. 1950s photograph. Its appearance is little changed, with windows placed in the front of the wing at left. (The Dorn's Collection.)

"Maplehurst" was built by Charles McDonald around 1880 at the northwest corner of Rumson Road and Tennis Court Lane. The architect of this Shingle Style house is unknown. It was owned by brewer Rudolph Erbshoh when pictured on a postcard c. 1910.

"Lauriston" is the historic name of the Colonial Revival tile and stucco house built for Henry A. Caesar on 91 Rumson Road and named for his wife Laura in 1910. It was designed by Red Bank and New York architect Leon Cubberley. The house once commanded block-long frontage and extensive acreage on all sides. Several farm buildings were on the grounds. Development has left only a narrow driveway on Rumson Road, with four newer houses on the former front lawn. An aerial photograph still provides the best view.

A spacious entrance hall is one of the outstanding architectural features of "Lauriston." The place was, perhaps, better known for its fine tree specimens and its many flower gardens, which contained plantings from around the world. Charles U. Caesar inherited the property and sold it to J. Howard Smith in 1942.

Fritz Achelis, a Brooklyn native born in 1843, worked in his family's wholesale dry goods business until leaving to head a hard-rubber company. His name is remembered in the well-known hard-rubber "Ace" comb. He built this Queen Anne-style country house, designed by architect H. Hudson Holly and erected by Sea Bright contractor Charles L. Walters, in 1889. Located on the south side of Rumson Road, west of Bingham Avenue, his estate once ran south to the Shrewsbury River and included numerous farm buildings. It is shown here c. 1910. (Collection of Michael Steinhorn.)

The house at 105 Rumson Road, now named "Riverlands," was remodeled by Red Bank architect Ernest A. Arend c. 1915 in the Colonial Revival style. Only slight reminders of the original design remain on this, the north facade, notably the porte-cochere. The front gable is now a modest dormer, one of seven in a built-out upper story. The south elevation, however, has not been remodeled and remains today in character with the style at the top of the page.

E. Gay Hamilton built the house at 108 Rumson Road c. 1867 when he bought 37 acres of A. Hance & Sons' Rumson Nurseries. It is an unusual example of a pre-1870 mansion, thus predating the Sea Bright Bridge, and an unusual Rumson Road Italianate-style house. The original house was expanded more than once, but the three-bay front reflects the original facade. A center tower, probably added after original construction, was later removed. The porches are likely later additions.

Two notable owners are associated with 108 Rumson Road: Robert Leighton Crawford and Rufus C. Finch. Crawford, a Civil War captain with the Confederate Army, likely made the major expansion in the rear, probably in the 1880s. Finch, a major figure in equine circles, bought the place in 1921 and probably had the outstanding Colonial Revival-influenced stairs built in the hall. The character of the splendid hall is intact, although the hand-painted wall paper no longer exists. (From the *Monmouth Pictorial*, Autumn-Winter, 1936.)

Hubert K. Dalton, a native of England and an engineer who founded a tool and die company that was merged into General Motors, built this Georgian Revival house named "Willowbrook" in 1931. His architect was Alfred Busselle of New York. Dalton was well known as a grower of orchids. He traveled extensively and moved to Hawaii in 1941. The house, expanded since construction, stands at 114 Rumson Road. Dalton's estate has been reduced by development, which is continuing at the time of this publication (1996).

Selmar Hess' barn was destroyed by fire in September 1899. E.E. Paul, a New York contractor, built this stable the following year. During the early years of the automobile age, it was reported as having the capacity for ten cars and fifteen horses.

Selmar Hess, born in Germany c. 1847, was a New York publisher. He was one of the first to sell books by subscription and to use photographs for illustrations. He bought the Clinton B. Fisk place on the north side of Rumson Road, which was later demolished to allow the construction of the house on the preceding page. He died in 1917.

The Selmar Hess family, consisting of Hesses and Elkuses, pose for a photograph in the dining room of their Rumson Road home, known as "Knollwood." Selmar was the father-in-law of Abram I. Elkus. One of Abram's granddaughters, Katherine Elkus, became mayor of Red Bank under her married name, White.

William F. Havemeyer, a member of the New York sugar trust family, built this large Queen Anne house with strong Tudor Revival elements on the north side of Rumson Road near Kemp Avenue in 1890. It was designed by Brunner and Tryon of New York. The wing at left, built on an angle, contained service facilities (including the kitchen), and a large hall dominated the main block. Two noteworthy later owners held the property: Colonel William Barbour, a Paterson textile manufacturer, and George V. Coe. Coe sold the property in 1946 to developer Harry S. Willey. (From *Seaside Souvenir*.)

Nathan F. Barrett designed the grounds of the Havemeyer estate known as "The Beeches." It contained a noteworthy Italian garden, also pictured in *Seaside Souvenir*. The main house was demolished, but several outbuildings were remodeled as private residences. The fine carriage house is a landmark in its own right.

The Robert Hance house at 128 Rumson Road at its northeast corner with Bellevue Avenue dates from *c.* 1845, despite its Colonial Revival appearance. Its Italianate-style origins are revealed by the tall first-story windows and historic mapping, which indicates a house has existed on the site from at least 1851. The two bays on the west, visible here, were added later. The triangular pedimented dormers are also later additions. The wall was built by H.L. Terrell in 1900. (The Dorn's Collection.)

This view between the Scott/Terrell house and the Hance house suggests the expansiveness of the property. The outbuildings and windmills are gone, with additional houses added to the site. These two and the following four pictures are from a single photograph session, believed to have taken place *c.* 1900. (The Dorn's Collection.)

John Hance, an original buyer of Rumson land in 1665, had holdings of about 500 acres. Robert Hance was a successful peach farmer who had abundant crops into the 1880s, by which time Rumson Road had its distinct country house make-up. The family also operated A. Hance & Son, Rumson Nurseries. The nursery was located west of the house and enjoyed a national business. (The Dorn's Collection.)

George S. Scott built a substantial country house in 1882. His carriage house, shown above, was later remodeled into a residence. A. Hance & Son, Rumson Nurseries ran into financial difficulty in the depression of 1873 and failed in 1878. Benjamin Hance later worked as a landscape architect associated with the famed Nathan Barrett, who laid out the Scott estate. (The Dorn's Collection.)

The *American Architect & Building News* of January 6, 1883 reads: "'Seacroft' is built of heavy framing with the walls lined and filled and made to resist the stormy exigencies of a very exposed position. The site is upon a high hill knoll commanding the ocean and a stretch of coast from Sandy Hook to Long Branch. The house is finished internally in butternut, the first floor is paneled, ceiled, and timbered in the same, with the rafters and beams moulded and carved."

Country houses were important in the diverse career of architect Bruce Price (1843–1903), notably the many he designed at Tuxedo Park, New York. The 1882 "Seacroft" is one of his most richly designed Queen Anne structures; its significance is reflected in the aforementioned architectural journal. A later, restrained early Colonial Revival is on p. 28. The house has been extensively remodeled, with the north elevation still resembling the original design. The once-extensive grounds have been subdivided, and construction in front of the house has taken away its Rumson Road address.

Scott owned the place a short ten years, selling in 1892 to Herbert Leslie Terrell, a Yale University and Albany Law School graduate who was active in railroad and mining interests. The south elevation was remodeled with a Mount Vernon-like appearance, a popular inspiration for Colonial Revival designs. The remodeling date and architect are unknown. Terrell died in 1909, with his wife's estate selling the property in 1926. This is a contemporary view visible from Rumson Road east of Bellevue Avenue.

The end-gabled roof over the porte-cochere, seen on the right, opposite, is visible behind the main block in this post-remodeling, pre-development aerial view. Allencrest Road, the house's present location, was opened from an estate drive, visible between the residence and the carriage house.

Jacob Henry Schiff was born 1847 in Germany, and emigrated to the United States in 1865. He became a citizen and a banker in 1870, but returned to Germany in 1872. He came back to New York in 1874 as a partner in Kuhn, Loeb & Company, a firm he headed by 1885. His career focused on railroad finance. Schiff may be best remembered for his philanthropic munificence, especially the gift of the Semitic Museum at Harvard c. 1900. Schiff married Therese Loeb in 1875 and died in 1920. This portrait is from John W. Leonard's 1910 *History of New York City*.

Jose F. de Navarro, a New York financier and native of Spain, bought a river-to-river plot of about 375 acres in 1878. He built this house at the northeast corner of Rumson Road and Buena Vista Avenue the next year. Jacob Schiff bought the house and nearly 50 acres running north to Ridge Road c. 1891. He improved the house, although the nature of the changes are not evident in documentary or pictorial evidence. It is shown here in a c. 1910 postcard view. (Collection of Michael Steinhorn.)

A second and probably later view of the above house suggests its nickname, "The Terraces," and is identified as the Loeb residence. The extended Schiff-Loeb family resided in at least two houses on the property. The other house, in mid-block between Rumson and Ridge Roads, had a laboratory on the grounds for Morris Loeb. It was demolished in the 1930s, a project recalled in recent years by a roofing worker, with the present one-story residence erected then. (Collection of Michael Steinhorn.)

The Schiff carriage house, with its distinctive clock tower, was built with a U-plan around 1900 at 59 Buena Vista Avenue. It was designed by E. Harris James in the French Norman style. Its precise origin is not clear, although the clock has a date of 1893. The Navarro estate that Schiff bought included the usual outbuildings, but the 1889 *Wolverton Atlas* does not indicate a structure on the site of the building pictured here. The building was converted to a year-round residence in the 1950s.

David B. Keeler built 76 Buena Vista Avenue in 1883. His architect was Edward L. Woodruff, who also designed the Ellesmere Park community in which the Keeler house was built. This house is often associated with a later owner, Thomas N. McCarter, who bought it in 1895. Although McCarter occupied it but briefly, he attracted his brothers nearby, establishing a Rumson link for what was arguably New Jersey's most powerful family. The house has been expanded, but its integrity has remained intact. It is shown here in a *c.* 1910 postcard view. (Collection of Michael Steinhorn.)

Uzal H. McCarter was born in 1861. He was educated at Princeton and in 1904 was elected president of the firm that in time became the Fidelity Union Trust Company. He hired Warrington G. Lawrence to design this two-and-one-half-story Colonial Revival house on the Rumson Road frontage of Ellesmere Park. It was built in 1903, a time when his brother still was his south border neighbor. McCarter sold the house in 1917 and moved to Red Bank, into the enormous Andrew Freedman house on Tower Hill. This is the present view of the north facade of 141 Rumson Road.

This view of the south elevation was taken from *Seaside Souvenir*. Early Ellesmere Park lots ran west to Conover Avenue, which provided a rear entrance to the houses. The porch, shown here as built, overlooked several outbuildings on the property. It was removed in the 1970s. New York and Rumson architect George Rudolph designed a replica, using this picture as a guide. The porch was faithfully rebuilt in 1993, reflecting the major commitment to historic fidelity by the present owners Morgan Cline and Ben D'Onofrio.

Robert McCarter's house—"Tall Trees"—at the southwest corner of Rumson Road and Conover Avenue was built in 1902, around the same time as his brother Uzal's. The two are separated by the historic Rumson Cemetery. Warrington G. Lawrence , the family's architect, is known to have designed outbuildings and alterations for Robert McCarter, and he probably designed the house as well. McCarter, a former state attorney general, was described as the dean of New Jersey's bar when he died in 1941. The picture is contemporary.

Ellesmere Park, one of two designed communities laid out in 1882, was located south of Rumson Road and west of Buena Vista Avenue. Its presiding architect was Edward L. Woodruff of Staten Island; Nathan Barrett of New York designed the grounds. Georgiana and William Shedd of New York hired Rossiter and Wright of New York to design this Shingle Style house with Colonial Revival influence. It was completed in 1892 and stands at 82 Buena Vista Avenue.

Charles B. and Marion Choate Harding assembled an 18.5-acre tract from Thorton Realty and Thomas N. McCarter in 1925, building this substantial Colonial Revival house not long thereafter. (Collection of Michael Steinhorn.)

Dr. Edwin F. Stewart bought 12 acres from Thomas N. McCarter at the northwest corner of Rumson and Fair Haven Roads in 1925 and hired Alfred Busselle to design this Tudor Revival house. Its date, location (on the borough's western stem of Rumson Road), and scale (with three bedrooms and three rooms for staff), reflect the transition of the Rumson estate area from summer houses to year-round living. The house stands, although the lot has been reduced through development. Stewart achieved the distinction of being the oldest living Eagle Scout at his death in 1915.

Hiram S. Thomas, a native of Canada, rented the John Home house on the northwest corner of Rumson and Hance Roads in 1896 for the opening of a road house. From early experience serving on steamers, Thomas operated or served in restaurants and clubs at Chicago, Saratoga (where he originated Saratoga chips), Washington, D.C., and Lakewood, NJ. Alternately known as the Rumson Inn or Thomas' Inn, it was located in what became Little Silver, and was opened before either municipality was formed. It is shown here in a c. 1905 postcard view.

By 1890 Rumson Road was one of the finest country drives in America. Its upkeep and beauty were largely the result of the Rumson Road Association's efforts, led by Edward Kemp. This old thoroughfare was built to connect Shrewsbury and Black Point, having earlier taken a northerly course to Navesink Avenue. It was extended east to the Shrewsbury River after the 1870 opening of the Sea Bright Bridge. Sections of the road were lighted in 1903, and turned over to the county in 1904. Rumson Road was paved in concrete in 1919, a few years after this postcard view was taken.

The average viewer of this still-standing gate likely presumes it is a private entrance to a private club. However, the actual entry to the club is some distance to the south. The gate is on a public road, Clubway, that constitutes the eastern border of the Rumson Park neighborhood. Note the "Park" on the west (right) post. Rumson Park and the Rumson Country Club were developed simultaneously, both properties bought in 1908 by groups led by Edward Dean Adams.

Ivins Creek separated the Rumson Park property from the land of Annie Millward. Millward entered an agreement in 1909 permitting the former to make the creek navigable. The developers built the Rumson Waterway, seen here from its Shrewsbury River outlet, which borders Buttonwood Lane properties on the east. The Millward property was developed in the 1930s, with the house lots bordering the Waterway on the west.

The western elevation (shown here in the 1970s) of 10 Buttonwood Lane reflects the Colonial Revival style, a stylistic impression even more evident on the east. However, the house's origin is uncovered in an older main block, visible behind the columns. An older house, c. 1880s, earlier standing in Monmouth Beach, was moved here by barge, perhaps around 1922. Large Colonial Revival additions were made, enveloping the older house, which has signs of its older origins inside.

The Rumson Country Club opened their new clubhouse on July 2, 1910, with golf and a polo match between the Meadowbrook and visiting Rockaway teams, won by the former. The club was a consolidation of the Rumson Polo Club, Meadow Yacht Club, and the Sea Bright Golf Club. The Herbert Polo Field, named for the father of the game in the United States, was in front of the clubhouse, the bowling and tennis courts were in the rear, and the golf course laid out by Walter J. Travers was to the west. This is a c. 1910 postcard. (Collection of Michael Steinhorn.)

The clubhouse, shown here c. 1920, was designed by George Freeman of New York in the Tudor Revival style, while the grounds were laid out by Charles W. Leavitt, who was also landscape architect for club director J. Amory Haskell's famed estate in Middletown Township. The two-and-one-half-story building was about 200 feet in length and 75 feet wide. The building was destroyed by fire on February 7, 1945. (Collection of Michael Steinhorn.)

The house at 178 Rumson Road was built in 1909 by Thomas Tyndall Jr., on a farm formerly owned by his father, a Dublin native born of English parents. The original house, a Colonial Revival with a wraparound porch, had six rooms on the first floor and five on the second. It was remodeled by J. Ford Johnson in 1929 and severely damaged by fire in 1930. Johnson, a leading polo player, liked the locale across from the county club's polo fields. He lent the house to the club for temporary use while the clubhouse was being rebuilt after a 1945 fire.

An element of surprise preceded the taking of this prize polo picture in June 1947. A charging horse outside the polo field caused George Moss to roll over for self-preservation. He came forward with camera ready, snapped quickly, and only after developing discovered he had captured Hubert (Rube) Williams' horse with four hooves airborne and the ball in flight. For the technically minded, it was Kodak Plus-X at 1/400.

While contemplating options for a new clubhouse, including the possibility of rebuilding, the William E. Strong house at "The Point" on the Shrewsbury River became available. Then owner Edward W. Scudder, publisher of the *Newark Evening News*, was selling the land for development. The house would have to be moved. It was divided into three parts, with one major section relocated to 121 Avenue of Two Rivers. It remains there as a private residence. (The Dorn's Collection.)

The building was cut at a joint where a wing one-third the size of the central section had been added to the original structure. Progress was slow, and at times was halted by heavy rains that made the swampy area unworkable. The smaller central section, which can be seen in this picture next to the larger one, was floated in June 1946 to its new site without mishap. Problems were encountered with the larger central section, which measured 42-by-72 feet, shown in the Shrewsbury River in the top picture. (The Dorn's Collection.)

The barge carrying the larger central section struck a sandbar. It was stuck there, having to await the next full high tide. It reached land, of course, and the two central sections were joined. (It seems appropriate to be writing this caption in April 1996 as Philip Glass' *The Voyage* is being broadcast.) The two sections were moved 1,500 feet on land to the new location. The club hired New York architects Polhemus and Coffin, who had numerous country house commissions in the area, to supervise re-erection. (The Dorn's Collection.)

The larger section is shown here at its point of separation. Reconstruction overran its budget. The destroyed building had been underinsured, contributing to fiscal crisis. A mortgage and the sale of bonds helped complete the project. The new clubhouse opened on May 3, 1947. (The Dorn's Collection.)

Jonathan P. Cooper bought about 125 acres of John S. Leonard's farm in 1877. He promptly built this three-story Second Empire-style house. Personal tragedy surrounded Cooper's family. His wife, who died prematurely, was likely poisoned, and a family nurse drank poison, but did not die. The family's adopted daughter was suspected in the poisonings; she and her husband both died young as well. The stature of the house was reflected in a full-page plate in the 1878 Woolman and Rose *Historical and Biographical Atlas of the New Jersey Coast*, the source of this image.

The house at 21 Hance Road was inherited by Lily May Borden, Jonathan Cooper's young granddaughter. It eventually had to be sold to satisfy a tax lien. The building fronts Rumson Road, but the once large farm has been intensively developed and newer houses were built in front of it. The mansard roof is distinguished by its paired, high, narrow windows in the center dormer. The house was later owned by Charles Doelger, a New York brewer, who probably added many of the interior Colonial Revival decorative elements.

Three
Oceanic Bridge
and Village

Transport by steamboat was fundamental in the growth of the Oceanic section of Rumson. An earlier dock was at the foot of Washington Street, as noted on the map on the next page. It was relocated one block to the west to Lafayette Street to permit construction of the Oceanic Bridge landing at Washington Street. The 165-foot *Albertina*, built in 1882 and operated by the Merchants Steamboat Company, was, along with its sister ship, the *Sea Bird*, one of the two most prominent vessels on the Navesink River run. It is shown here at the Lafayette Street dock c. 1920.

The lots of Thomas G. Hunt's 1853 land auction made up much of the settled village for a long while. Hunt built the Port Washington Pavilion Hotel in 1845 to enhance the area for vacationers, who would presumably travel on his steamboat. The illustrations on the full-size original are exceptional, the one at right showing detail on the opposite river shore. (The Dorn's Collection.)

The river shore was well developed by the time the 1873 *Beers Atlas of Monmouth County* was published. On the right (east) is the northern end of Parmly's river-to-river estate, spelled incorrectly. An early school just off southeast corner of the map was moved and remodeled as a residence. No picture is available of Martinus Bergen's canning factory. Note that the numbered streets ran only the block north from River Road, shown here as the Red Bank Road, to the water.

This building was erected as the first Lafayette Street School in 1879. It was replaced on the same site in 1893 by the brick school on p. 69. The building was moved one-half block east on the south side of Church and became Red Men's Hall, the home of a social/fraternal organization. Shown here c. 1880, it is now Donald Pitman's residence and metal plating shop. (The Dorn's Collection.)

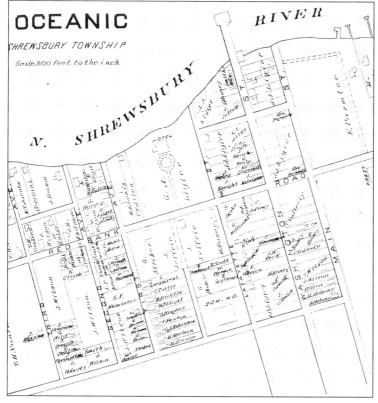

The principal change from the 1873 plan reflected in this 1889 Oceanic village map is the development of the Martinus Bergen tract south of West River Road (shown as Red Bank Road) and west of Lafayette Street. The school was then on the site of his canning factory. Houses filled much of the new streets, some having been moved from other sites, with one example on p. 73.

Bingham Hall is the present name of the Greek Revival-style Port Washington Church built by Thomas Hunt and dedicated in 1842. Hunt developed the surrounding area following a land purchase of about 100 acres in 1840, and recognized a need for a place to worship. He also built a hotel, store, and dock, which are no longer extant. After initial use by varied Protestant denominations, this edifice was acquired by the Presbyterians in 1861, who occupied it until the church below was built. The borough acquired the building for use as a community center in 1942.

Rumson Presbyterians built their own church in 1886. This fine early work in the Shingle Style was designed by famed New York architect Thomas Hastings, the son of his namesake, a regular guest clergy at the church. Its many distinctive architectural features contribute to the structure's landmark stature, including its patterned wood shingles, port cochere, colonnade, and octagonal tower with a hexagonal steeple. This is the south facade that faces River Road, east of Bingham Avenue.

The land for the church was donated by Ehrick Parmly. Note the hipped dormers in the tower and the round arch windows, a design motif repeated throughout. Hastings' design was unusual for church architecture, but his tradition-breaking arrangement incorporated materials and a style consistent with his other work of the time in the area. This is the rear of the church at 4 East River Road.

The interior of the First Presbyterian Church of Rumson is as richly decorated as the exterior, containing stained-glass windows on each wall, most of them memorials. The interior walls are clad in scalloped shingles throughout. The nave is separated from a side aisle by Corinthian columns.

After a three-year contest over cost, location, and type of draw, the still-unfinished Oceanic Bridge connecting Rumson to the Locust section of Middletown Township opened to public traffic on Memorial Day, May 30, 1891. The bridge, shown here c. 1910, was built by Dean and Westbrook, the county's favorite bridge builders of the day. It immediately attracted considerable traffic, both vehicle and pedestrian, the absence of a footpath notwithstanding.

The crew on an open draw is awaiting passage of the *Sea Bird*, c. 1905. The pivot draw drew vocal opposition, with its location a second issue. The site was close to the Rumson shore. A human crew winding the mechanical gears did not facilitate quick opening and closing of the draw. (Collection of John Rhody.)

Washington Street looking north from its Hunt Street intersection around 1910 reveals the Oceanic Bridge in the distance. A boarding house is on the left (west) side, while at right is a gatepost to the driveway of the Samuel Crooks house (see p. 72). The old Port Washington Hotel, later the Shrewsbury Inn (see pp. 78 and 79), is in the right background. (Collection of Michael Steinhorn.)

The block south of the view at top, between River Road and Hunt Street, reveals a no-longer-standing Second Empire house on the west side of Washington Street at a time when a horse was the principal means of travel. Note the stepping stone at left. (Collection of John Rhody.)

Monmouth Electric Company car No. 26, *c.* 1910, is shown going east on River Road at Allen Street in front of Striker's store, which at the time contained the post office. Note the three-story building a block to the west on the southwest corner of First Street, a large apartment known as "The Flats." It was demolished *c.* 1916, and the site was purchased for the Church of the Holy Rosary. (Collection of John Rhody.)

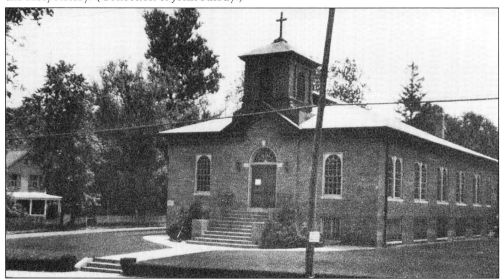

Holy Cross Church bought the southeast corner of River Road and Second Street in 1916. The church was unable to acquire the remainder of the block until 1919, when it purchased the Vanderbeek property on the southwest corner of River and First. This simple but attractive Colonial Revival edifice, shown here in the 1920s, was built in 1923 and dedicated on July 1. It was named the Church of the Holy Rosary. It served western Rumson until 1994, when the still well-preserved church was closed. (Collection of Michael Steinhorn.)

The 1893 Lafayette Street School was built on the same southwest corner of Church and Lafayette Streets where the earlier school stood (see p. 63). It is at times identified as the "high school," but instruction here included only the ninth and tenth grades, in addition to the elementary grades. Students seeking completion of high school went elsewhere, typically Red Bank, until the final two years were added in 1933. Tennis courts are on the site now. This view is from a c. 1903 postcard. (Collection of Michael Steinhorn.)

The Goodwill Methodist Church was organized in 1877, with this edifice built that year at the southwest corner of River Road and Washington Street on a lot sold by Sarah Midwinter on "easy" terms. The Gothic Revival church, shown here c. 1908, was moved to Washington Street in 1923 and was damaged by fire in the 1940s. The congregation diminished and in the early 1960s it merged with Christ Church-United Methodist in Fair Haven. A store is now on the site. (Collection of John Rhody.)

The horse and carriage would soon compete on River Road with the trolley. This *c.* 1903 postcard, pre-dating the laying of the tracks, shows the same corner with Allen Street that is pictured below. (Collection of Michael Steinhorn.)

This *c.* 1910 view, looking east to the south side of West River Road at Allen Street, shows the old Oceanic Hook & Ladder Company firehouse (at center), built in 1890 on the east corner. Striker's store (at right) was built in 1887 by local contractor William Pearsall and mason James P. Bruce. (Collection of Michael Steinhorn.)

Oceanic Hook & Ladder Company No. 1 replaced their fifty-year-old frame firehouse with this stucco-clad Moderne design by J. Sanford Shanley, a Rumsonian architect whose office was in Newark. Former mayor W. Warren Barbour, then a U.S. senator, is shown here speaking at the cornerstone laying on December 31, 1939. The company held its first meeting there on April 3, 1940. (The Dorn's Collection.)

This 1920s postcard shows the Oceanic Free Library, given to the people of Rumson by Henry E. Meeker as a memorial to his son William, who was killed in a training accident in France while serving with the Lafayette Flying Corps. Thomas Hastings designed this small brick building on the southwest corner of River Road and Second Street. The library opened in 1921. The Methodist parsonage can be seen to the west of the library. The library, needful of additional space, moved to East Oceanic in 1959. (Collection of Michael Steinhorn.)

Joseph Strohmenger had a bottling plant in his barn on the south side of his house lot at 85 Lafayette Street. His early bottles are stamped "1890" and "Turtle Bay Lager Beer"; later bottles include the brewery owner's name, Fred Opporman Jr. The name is not visible on this quintet's bottles, but we just know what they are drinking.

Samuel Crooks, an Irish immigrant in the coffee-tea trade, built this 1907 house, designed by Leon Cubberley and erected by Wooley & Burchell, on the block surrounded by Bingham, Hunt, and Washington. It is a Four Square with attractive Colonial Revival decoration, described when new as "one of the ornaments of Oceanic," by the *New Jersey Standard*. Crooks died in 1918. The house, shown here *c.* 1910, was demolished in the 1970s, with an office building on the block now. (Collection of John Rhody.)

The well-preserved outhouse at 19 Church Street suggests one should look closely at the house before presuming it was originally constructed in 1870s Second Empire style. The Martinus Bergen property was developed in the 1870s, a time when one might have expected indoor plumbing in a substantial house. The present owners, the Robert Hills, were told that the house had been removed from the shore. Examination of the house indicated the mansard-roofed upper story had been added after construction and that an older Greek Revival dwelling indeed had been moved. Now used for garden storage, this rare surviving outhouse has earned a formal title, "The Oceanic Necessary."

This house at 19 Church Street is the T.H. Van Tine house, shown as the westernmost shore property on the map on the bottom of p. 62. The property was purchased by M.C.D. Borden in 1901, with the existing buildings sold to buyers who would move them without disturbing the landscaping. The house's proportions, windows, and door enframement are characteristic of Greek Revival architecture. A search of Van Tine's deed revealed he bought the property from Archibald Haviland in 1858, a date also on the back of a mantel. Greek Revival architecture was nearing the end of a long spell of fashion then.

This c. 1860s house and old garage still sit on the Navesink River shore, west of Victory Park.

Fishing near the Oceanic Bridge was and is a pleasant pastime.

Long Point is a spit of land reaching into the Navesink River outside 80 West River Road. Its extension into the river is best viewed from the top of the hill on the Middletown north shore. This is a *c.* 1920 postcard. (Collection of Michael Steinhorn.)

The tracks were removed in 1943, two decades after the trolley stopped running. The steel had become valuable as war-time scrap. Ed Kemble captured the removal process on May 28, 1943. The author was two weeks old that day and had not yet begun to think about historical matters.

James Enright built the store at the northeast corner of River Road and Lafayette Street in 1887. It was constructed by contractor W.A. Jeffery, and at 22-by-50 feet, it was one of the largest buildings in the village. It was long-owned by William Fogelson, who sold his drugstore and realty to William and Frances Statter in 1974 and 1978 respectively. The store, shown here c. 1930, was expanded to the east in 1983 and is today's Rumson Pharmacy. (Collection of Michael Steinhorn.)

West River Road and Allen Street was obviously a charming spot early in the century judging by the frequency of its illustrations. Having been seen on p. 70 with horse and carriage and trolley, it is shown here with a horse-drawn sprinkler. Nostalgic about the not-so-good old days? Remember, the streets were alternately dusty and muddy, with the horse having its own environmental cost.

The early site of the Goodwill Methodist Church (see p. 69) is shown here c. 1950, occupied by a brick store. Arend's ice cream parlor-luncheonette filled the corner then. The adjacent post office was still on the village's main street, a location later made more difficult to access by growing traffic. (Collection of Michael Steinhorn.)

This late-1940s view shows the predecessor of the gas station still on the southwest corner of Allen Street and River Road. At right is a standard "domestic"-style building popular in the 1920s, designed not unlike a small cottage, the better to fit in a respectable streetscape. The service bays were added and the station replaced with a larger, later design. (The Dorn's Collection.)

Hunt's Pavilion Hotel, shown here *c.* 1915, was operated by a number of owners and managers. Victor Ligier conducted it for many years during the late nineteenth and early twentieth centuries. The hotel had about forty rooms and was known by various names, including Rumson Inn and Shrewsbury Inn. The smaller building at left, with about twelve rooms, was part of the hotel property and operation.

The cottage at top is barely visible in this *c.* 1915 postcard of the Shrewsbury Inn's dock. The hotel is adjacent to the east of the old Oceanic Bridge, occupying the block between Bingham and Washington on the east and west, and Hunt Street and the Navesink River on the south and north.

The site on the opposite page was among Rumson's most frequently illustrated locales early in this century. It can be recognized in this *c.* 1950 view placing it adjacent to the west of the present Oceanic Bridge. The cottage became the residence of the Walshes, who bought the inn. William Augustine photographed this scene for Father Henry C. Beck to illustrate an article on Fair Haven. (Special Collections and Archives, Rutgers University Libraries.)

The hotel was demolished *c.* 1960 to allow the construction of the River House restaurant. By the time this 1960s aerial view was taken, its name had been changed to Fisherman's Wharf. Note Washington Street, the passage to the old Oceanic Bridge, ending at the river. As this book goes to print in May 1996, the magnificently sited building has been closed for re-development.

The Oceanic Bridge was in poor condition by the mid-1930s. A 10 mph speed limitation was mandated in 1937 to reduce the risk of the collapse of the bridge, which was buckled at each end and which moved to a dangerous extent. A key factor in the timing of the replacement was the securing of federal funding, which was granted in 1938. This September 1939 photograph of the construction scene was taken while looking toward the Rumson shore. (Collection of John Rhody.)

The new bridge, located one block to the east of the old bridge, was built 1939–40, while the old span, visible to the right, was still in use. Bingham Avenue became the new bridge access street. Fred T. Ley & Company of New York was awarded the contract with a low bid of $997,298 as part of a projected cost of around $1,150,000, for which the Public Works Administration granted $513,000. The job's local engineer was Lionel W. Lancaster. This photograph was also taken looking toward Rumson. (Collection of John Rhody.)

The location of the draw was an issue. It was proposed relocating it from close to the Rumson shore to near the center of the river, a process that would improve navigation, enhance bridge esthetics, and increase the cost. The new location was approved and a new channel dug. The bascule draw was also lengthened and the bridge built higher over the water. This view of the draw is looking west. (Collection of John Rhody.)

The new bridge opened on the afternoon of March 16, 1940. Several officials and builder representatives met at the middle of the still-unfinished span. A dedication and ceremony was planned for May, but the job fell consistently behind. An event scheduled for Memorial Day was put off on May 22. One can not spot the outstanding work in this view, taken on June 1, 1940, looking toward the Middletown shore. (Collection of John Rhody.)

Bertram Borden purchased parcels in 1919 from the Ligier and Brown estates for establishing a public park; frontages were 300 feet on the River Road and the Navesink River and 500 feet on Lafayette Street. The *Register* of December 3, 1919, said this of the latter property: "The Brown property in recent years has been rented during the summer months by visitors from New York and other large cities who put up tents and bungalows on the place . . . The more staid residents of Rumson looked askance at the acts of some of these summer visitors . . . there is a general feeling of thankfulness . . . it will mean a different use for the property." This is a *c.* 1918 postcard. (Collection of John Rhody.)

Victory Park, dedicated July 4, 1920, was named to honor those who served in World War I. A memorial listed the names of seven Rumsonians who lost their lives in the war: Samuel H. Compton, George Halton, Dominic Lagroteria, William H. Meeker, Ellesworth Rex, John Nelson, and Edward Reid. Among the listed returning veterans was John C. Borden, a nephew of the donors of the memorial. The Mary Owen Borden Memorial Foundation conveyed the park to the Borough of Rumson by a deed dated December 19, 1947. (Collection of Michael Steinhorn.)

Four
Oceanic Estates

Christmas at "Old Oaks" was a major celebration. Howard Borden had a flair for exotic entertainments and the unusual. Note the small figures, photographs cut to shape and mounted on cut-wood forms. This is a *c.* 1920s view.

Matthew C. Borden was born July 28, 1843, in Fall River, Massachusetts, son of leading manufacturer Richard Borden. He entered the dry goods trade, after graduating from Yale in 1864, in time representing the American Print Works as selling agent. After that company failed, he reorganized it as The American Printing Company, and as sole owner, built up an enormous fabric manufacturing business. Borden also maintained a distribution firm, increasing his power and influence in the world of cloth. He died on May 27, 1912.

"Old Oaks," the residence of Howard Borden, is believed to have originated as the home of his father, Matthew. It no longer stands, impeding study. This c. 1917 photograph shows the side containing an indoor pool, with alterations designed by George S. Chappell.

The Borden carriage house is in the background of this c. 1918 view of the brick gate posts to the Borden residential property. Both structures still stand on the north side of River Road, west of Third Street.

The Borden carriage house at 85 West River Road was built in 1889, designed by Thomas Hastings, a major New York architect. It is Shingle Style, with Richardsonian Romanesque elements. Hastings' father, president of New York's Union Theological Seminary, had a summer house nearby and was a frequent guest clergy at the Rumson Presbyterian Church (also designed by the younger Hastings; see pp. 64 and 65). The carriage storage room has a scalloped shingle interior compatible with the interior of the church (see p. 65).

Cornelius N. Bliss, born 1833 in Fall River, Massachusetts, probably had a family tie to M.C.D. Borden, as his mother was Irene Borden Bliss. The two had business ties in the dry goods commission house of Bliss, Fabyan & Company, and at one time shared a house. Bliss was an active Republican, serving for some years as treasurer of the party's national committee. He served two years as secretary of the interior, and was photographed here while in that office. Bliss declined William McKinley's offer of the vice-presidency in 1900. He died in 1911.

Cornelius N. Bliss' house stood on a 30-acre plot on the north side of River Road, west of the Borden property. He held an additional 60 acres of farmland south of River Road. Howard S. Borden bought the property in late 1914 after it had been on the market for nearly three years. Several buildings were on the property. The house appears not to exist now, but analysis of the Bliss property will require the discovery of a detailed plat plan. (From *Seaside Souvenir*.)

Dr. Henry E. Owen's house, on a sizable plot at the southeast corner of River Road and Bellevue Avenue, was illustrated in *Seaside Souvenir*. It apparently no longer stands. His daughter Mary married Bertram H. Borden.

The Borden boathouse, built in 1905, is shown here in 1917 with the old Oceanic Bridge in the background. A channel was dug to the boathouse when Matthew C.D. Borden's yacht, *The Little Sovereign,* was placed in service in 1911. It was the fastest steamer on the shore, easily beating the Central Railroad vessels. It's been said you could set your watch by the vessel's regular departure and that it did not need to sound its whistle for the bridge's draw to open.

Bertram H. Borden was born in 1868. He joined the family business—The American Printing Company and its sales arm, M.C.D. Borden and Sons—at age twenty, and became president when his father died in 1912. He married Mary Owen. Bertram Borden is best known, indeed revered, for his many public benefactions, such as Victory Park (p. 82), the Mary Owen Borden Wing of Monmouth Medical Center, the Rumson High School stadium, and the Mary Owen Borden Carillon at Saint George's Church (p. 121). Bertram was photographed in a contented avuncular role with niece Edith in late 1954, nearly two years prior to his death.

Howard S. Borden was born c. 1877 and graduated from Yale in 1898. He was vice president of the family businesses and a director of Chemical Bank, but was better known for his other activities. Borden is pictured in his brigadier general's uniform c. 1921, when he attained leadership of the New Jersey National Guard. From thenceforth he was known as "The General." In 1906 he was made a local constable to help enforce speeding laws, but his favorite pursuits were yachting, flying, photography, and horsemanship, especially polo. He also built over 150 houses in Rumson, including the highly regarded developments of Old Farm Village in Oceanic and Pine Ridge (see p. 32). The general died in 1950.

Edith Caroline Curtis married Howard S. Borden on February 1, 1900 at Orange, New Jersey. Guests arrived by a special car attached to a Lackawanna train at Christopher and Barclay Street stations in New York. The couple likely met in Oceanic, where Edith visited the summer home of the cousins who gave her in marriage, Mr. and Mrs. Gardner Colby. A news brief a few months after the wedding mentioned the newlyweds, noting that "Mrs. Howard S. Borden is a remarkably attractive young woman . . ." This c. 1899 picture is labeled "A Good Joke."

The responsibilities of marriage and motherhood gave Edith C. Borden a more serious countenance. She is seen with her son William, born on October 22, 1915.

The best-known Borden boat, the steamer *The Little Sovereign*, is not pictured in this work, but the *Iris*, shown here *c*. 1917, was quite an impressive sailing vessel.

Howard S. Borden photographed at the wheel of the *Iris*, *c*. 1917.

Most of the Borden stable was devoted to polo. These prize-winning steeds, seen *c*. 1917, are presumed to be polo ponies.

Other Borden horses served in a variety of equine pastimes, including riding and carriage driving, activities to be illustrated in Volume II. "Arrow," the steed at right, caught the photographer in the act. His determined glare conveys that the photograph had better be flattering.

The organ at "Old Oaks," one of the finest in the county, was heavily damaged during a 1926 fire. It was rebuilt and placed over a concealed space that could be accessed by pressing an organ key (pressing the key opened a section of floor, providing access to a level below). The corridor at the bottom of the stairs contained dioramas with street scenes, and led to an open area suitable for parties.

The Rumson Bordens were not the dairy Bordens, this fine herd of cows notwithstanding. Gentlemen farmers early in this century were helpful in advancing the cause of sanitary dairy methods in an industry that was not then well-regulated, often lacking the standards we take for granted today.

"Old Oaks" was heavily damaged by fire on April 27, 1926. It was rebuilt, the new sections constructed of hollow tile. The unusual Christmas greeting appears to be 1926.

Efforts to sell "Old Oaks" after Howard Borden's death in 1950 were not successful. The house was demolished in the early 1950s, and a new house was built there in 1955. The garden in the left foreground is extant.

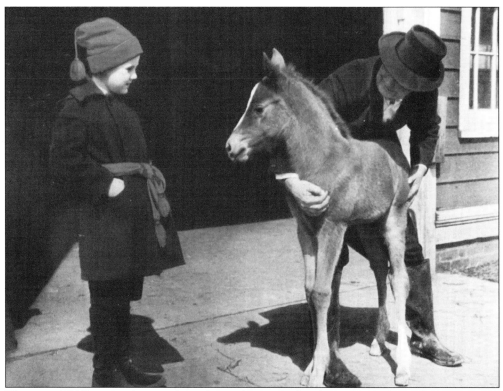

The young William Borden, a colt, and Joe Clancy, the head groom, are shown here *c.* 1921.

William Borden contemplates whether to continue sledding or not with his dog, *c.* 1921.

This pony is pulling a cart with Doris Borden (later Leonard) around 1918.

Doris Borden and brother William are shown at the piano c. 1930. William developed a serious interest in music, performing and arranging at a significant level for a young man through his college and military years. He was later an arranger for the noted band leader Claude Thornhill.

William H. Borden was a philosophy major at Princeton, where he was president of the Triangle Club, as they did not have a program then for his true love, music. He was a skilled piano and organ player, beginning formal music activity by organizing a dance band at Hotchkiss. William served as an officer in the family textile business, but later continued with music, owning a commercial recording business, Monmouth Evergreen Records. He is pictured with his young collies in the late 1940s. He died in 1988.

Mary Bruno, one of the first generation of her family born in the United States, married William Borden in 1950. At one time she worked in a New York hospital in cancer research. Mary and William Borden had two daughters, Edith and Vanna. This picture was taken in the summer of 1949.

An array of carriages once provided primary transportation on the Borden estate. The feeling of the belle époque is recreated generations later by Edith Borden, in a Borden carriage, with her sister Vanna seated to her left, and classmate Nancy Jones standing to her right.

Howard and Edith Borden at "Old Oaks" with their children John, Arthur, Doris, and William in the early 1920s. Their clothes reflect the fashion of the time, notably the long, heavy raccoon coats.

Matthew C.D. Borden built an extensive network of greenhouses at the eastern stem of his estate. Orchids were among the special plantings. He reportedly spent $100,000 on twenty-six structures in 1901.

Why is Third Street now offset 40 feet on the north side of River Road? Note the map on the bottom of p. 63, with the three numbered streets running straight to the river. Bertram Borden desired an extension of his lot for a side entrance when planning construction of his house. He purchased property east of the then-extant northern section of Third Street and arranged a land swap with the borough in 1919. (See Deed Book 1092, p. 58). A house once on the corner was moved a block to William Street.

Edwin Drexel Godfrey built this stucco-over-brick Italian Renaissance Revival house designed by Bosworth and Holden in 1907 as a summer home. Named "Popomora," the property consisted of 20 acres on a hill at River Road and Bellevue Avenue and about 2.5 acres running from the street to the river. Popomora was sold for development by a later owner in 1960. The house was demolished and eleven lots around today's Popomora Drive were carved from the plot. This is a c. 1910 postcard. Your collection needs both the red and green awning versions to be complete.

The Popomora estate, shown here c. 1910, included numerous outbuildings. One of them, the carriage house on the north side of River Road opposite Popomora Drive, has landmark stature. The grounds included various rose, formal, and rock gardens. (Collection of John Rhody.)

Joseph C. Hoagland, founder of the Royal Baking Powder Company, bought part of the Navarro estate in 1892 and had Shepley, Rutan, and Coolidge design this massive Tudor Revival house, named "Auldwood." The house was vacant during the 1930s depression, and the Borough of Rumson assumed ownership. It is seen here in a state of decline, photographed by Ed Kemble in 1943. It was demolished in 1947 and the surrounding property divided into nineteen lots in the area of 1.5 acres.

The residence at 4 Orchard Lane was once part of the Auldwood estate. Founder Joseph C. Hoagland died in 1899. His sons John and Raymond maintained the estate, expanding the structures to fit the needs of their "Rumson Farm" for breeding horses. This Shingle Style structure, formerly a combination stable and dwelling, is shown here in its present state.

Five

Around Town

The Parmlys long-held one of Rumson's greatest estates, the river-to-river Bingham Hill (see pp. 112–117). Lillian Parmly is shown here with her dog around 1915.

The East Oceanic primary school was built at East River and Black Point Roads in 1903. Only the first floor of a two-story building was occupied then, meeting the needs of the day. A 150-by-100-foot lot was bought from the McMahon property, with the school designed by Joseph Swannell of Red Bank. This view is from a c. 1910 postcard. (Collection of John Rhody.)

A trolley passes Black Point Road around 1910, with the East Oceanic School in the background. (Collection of Michael Steinhorn.)

Rumson education figures pose at an event at the Shadowbrook. They are, from left to right: Frances Noonan, unidentified, Laura Deane, Edna Johnson, unidentified, Evelyn Porter, Miss Pearsall (principal of Lafayette Street School), Marion Duckers (school nurse), and Marion Peseux.

Evelyn Porter (left) and Laura Deane (right) put faces behind the name of the Deane-Porter Elementary School. They flank Frances C. Noonan. The three women were photographed at a convention of the New Jersey Education Association in Atlantic City.

The Georgian-style main block of 16 Ridge Road likely dates from the mid-eighteenth century. The wing to the east (on the right) is probably older. The property is associated with several prominent owners, beginning with Lewis Morris of Passage Point. His cousin, also a Lewis Morris, was a royal governor and an apparent later owner. Seabury Tredwell, a New York merchant, used the place as a summer home prior to his death in 1865. His estate sold the vast holdings over the next four decades. This is an undated view of the south facade. (Collection of the Monmouth County Historical Association.)

The house has had major additions on each side since these views were taken. A living room was added *c.* 1930 by Harry Caesar to the west (on the right here, but on the left in the top photograph). A kitchen was added on the east, while an office was placed on the rear, or north elevation. Although the 600-acre estate has been reduced to 6, the house sits on a wooded lot, behind a pond, reminiscent of a time when this Rumson country seat had a commanding presence on the landscape. (Collection of the Monmouth County Historical Association.)

Robert L. Maitland built 87 Ridge Road in 1891–92, an outstanding transition house embracing late Shingle Style and early Colonial Revival elements. The architect is possibly the office of Edward L. Woodruff of Staten Island, based on evidence of a plat plan and building contract, although the latter indicates the project was supervised by Daniel Campbell of Staten Island. This image is from a c. 1910 postcard, produced at a time when the house was occupied by well-known owner Charles D. Halsey. (Collection of John Rhody.)

A recent picture of "Briarwood" indicates that its integrity remains intact although the east porch was removed. The bay window in the library at front left is curved glass, one of many fine architectural details. The house is readily visible on a high hill, but it can easily be missed while traveling Ridge Road below it. The once large property was subdivided, with Briarwood Road running through the former estate. The Charles Halseys bought the house in 1906. Charles served as a Rumson councilman, upholding then-current standards of decency and beginning a long legal encounter with James D. Allgor. (See pp. 22–25.)

Edward Dean Adams employed architects McKim, Mead, and White for the design of a major industrial facility, the Niagara Power Company's generating station. He bought his New York residence, a unit in the Villard Houses that the firm designed, and had that firm design his country house, the famed "Rohallion," built at 45 Bellevue Avenue in 1887. "Rohallion" was designed in the Shingle Style, as it appears here, but after repeated remodelings and expansions, the present building bears no resemblance to the original structure.

The "Rohallion" carriage house was placed north of the main dwelling, located at today's 8 North Rohallion Drive. It, too, was designed in the Shingle Style and was built with a clock tower resembling one in McKim, Mead, and White's well-known Newport (Rhode Island) casino. The carriage house was damaged by fire in 1897, and an early 1960s fire destroyed a wing of a former U-plan building. This picture probably predates the 1897 fire, with the present house much altered.

Edward Kemp bought Rumson Hill from George DeHaert Gillespie in 1879, having occupied the place since 1868. He eventually accumulated around 500 acres. Kemp retained the farm's old buildings, renovating them as necessary. This view reveals Kemp's expansion of a house of unknown origin. Kemp was known locally for his philanthropy; he raised funds for the first Sea Bright Bridge and was responsible more than any other person for making Rumson Road the splendid country drive it became. Although Rumson Hill is associated historically with its next owner, Kemp deserves to be remembered as one of Rumson's most influential residents. (From *Seaside Souvenir*.)

The only pre-McCarter Rumson Hill building still standing is the farmer's house at 15 Fair Haven Road. It also pre-dates Kemp, having belonged to George DeHaert Gillespie, a prominent New York hardware merchant, bank director, and sometime president of the Manhattan Bank. The house consists of an older section on the east (to the left), perhaps c. 1830, with the right section of the main block probably built around the time of Kemp's purchase. The house was extensively renovated in 1954, when Rumson Hill was being subdivided.

McCarter demolished the Kemp house, building this massive brick three-and-one-half-story house designed by Warrington G. Lawrence in the Georgian Revival style. It was built of deep red brick, laid in Flemish bond with terra-cotta and Indiana limestone trim and a copper roof. Its measurements were 129-by-60 feet. The press reported that he might call the place Rumson Haven, to combine Rumson Road and Fair Haven, but McCarter obviously retained the older name of Rumson Hill. This view is from a c. 1907 postcard photographed by Charles D. Chandler, and lent by his great-granddaughter, Marilyn Willis.

A newspaper photograph is sufficient to reflect the majesty of the hall of Rumson Hill. Thomas N. McCarter raised Rumson grandeur to new heights. His presence was also significant as he became in 1905 the first major city figure to make Rumson his permanent year-round residence (he came from Newark). The McCarters sold the property in 1951 and Rumson Hill was subdivided in 1954. The house was demolished ten years later; its substantial construction resulted in a difficult demolition project.

The Thomas McCarter house at Rumson Hill is viewed here *c.* 1940s in relationship to the now-removed Ridge Road bridge, seen above the house to the right. The tree-lined driveway is now Sycamore Lane. Note the absence of construction at the intersection of Ridge and Fair Haven Roads, top left. McCarter's garage/carriage house is at lower right. McCarter bought the property in 1904; his estate would span Rumson and Fair Haven, Ridge Road being the border at this point. (The Dorn's Collection.)

McCarter's Ridge Road arch, as it was called during construction, was built in 1915, designed by Brinley and Holbrook. The project included regrading the road, which left a clearance that later fell short of safety needs. Although the height warning in this view is 10 feet 6 inches, later pictures indicated it as 8 feet. Obviously, it depended where one measured. Calls for its removal were made since 1955; in 1988, many accidents later, the bridge was removed. With it went a modern graffiti tradition. This view is from the 1970s. Where are you now, Little Mary Sunshine?

This aerial view shows two of the no-longer-standing great estates prior to the post-World War II development of western Rumson. Thomas McCarter's Rumson Hill runs diagonally across the center of the photograph, the house close to the fold at center. McCarters Pond, in Fair Haven, is below the airplane's strut, with much of the curving driveway, today's Buttonwood Drive. Fair Haven Road runs from the street to its intersection with Rumson Road at bottom. McCarter's farm complex is on the east side. The brick gate posts are barely visible in front of a road leading to the still-standing farmer's house (see p. 107), although most farm structures are gone. Opposite the farm is the Edwin Stewart house (see p. 53). The Thomas Tindall place (see

p. 57) is the full house at lower left, while the house to its west, demolished in 1994, is only partially visible. Between them are houses owned by Harding, Churchill, and Atha around the time of the c. 1940s photograph. The gate to Rumson Park and the Rumson Country Club is represented by three white dots to the left of the golf course. The Havemeyer house (p. 43) is visible at center-right. Fellow drivers, notice the Oceanic Bridge in its usual summer position. Below it appears to be the Schiff house, but its still-standing outbuildings are inexplicably not visible. "Auldwood" (see p. 100) can barely be seen above and to the right of Schiff's. (The Dorn's Collection.)

"Bingham Hill" commands an elevation on the east side of Bingham Avenue at number 139. William Bingham, a key Revolutionary War financier, purchased in 1791 an old farmhouse and about 200 acres. He expanded the residence, using it not only as a retreat from the Philadelphia heat, but twice as a refuge from smallpox epidemics. This view is a Pach photograph, probably dating to the late nineteenth century, of the south facade. The octagonal wings, dating from Bingham's time, convey a recognizable impression today. This porch, a likely nineteenth-century addition, has been replaced by one spanning the wings.

The north elevation is likely unrecognizable today; a large, postmodern entry porch replaced the modest stairway shown in this c. 1900 photograph. The tower is also gone, with a garage constructed to the east. The property was purchased by Eleazar Parmly (see p. 114), who expanded the estate to run from river-to-river. The property passed to his son Ehrick, a dentist. Dalton Parmly purchased the property from his father's estate in 1911 and began breaking it up. Mike Jacobs, the noted prize-fight promoter, was a later owner. This is one of the two most important houses in Rumson, with the other on p. 104. (Collection of the Monmouth County Historical Association.)

The barn in Parmly's time was said to have been able to hold 100 tons of hay. Also noteworthy is the rotary windmill. Parmly had an extensive livestock and crop operation. Chickens and ducks were raised for sale to restaurants including Thomas' Inn and the Rumson Country Club. This photograph was taken c. 1920.

In 1885, when Ehrick Parmly built the house that became 65 Ridge Road, it was part of a vast river-to-river family estate, Bingham Hill, with the two major houses connected by a common driveway. The house, designed by New York architect Frederick B. White, is a fine, richly decorated example of Shingle Style architecture. The photograph dates from 1970, prior to the house parcel's subdivision. The house is hardly visible now from the road.

Eleazar Parmly was a major figure in nineteenth-century dentistry. He was born in Vermont in 1797 and spent a short time with a newspaper. After working in the west as an itinerant dentist, Parmly studied in Paris and entered partnership with his brother Levi in London in 1819 before beginning a forty-five-year practice of dentistry in New York. He founded the first dental periodical, the *American Journal of Dental Science*. Parmly died in New York in 1874 and is buried in the Rumson cemetery. This is a *c.* 1860s J.C. Buttre engraving from a Jaquith photograph.

Dalton Parmly was born in New York *c.* 1873, son of Ehrick Parmly. He owned the family Rumson property, developing part of it and being active as a real estate broker. Dalton opened Parmly Park, the neighborhood east of Bingham Avenue, between River and Ridge Roads. He is shown here at the Bingham Hill well house *c.* 1920.

John Parmly, son of Dalton, developed a professional interest in game and fish, in time opening a sporting goods shop in Sea Bright. He is seen *c.* 1935 with two groundhogs.

Lillian Parmly, holding her son John around 1918, helps provide a closer view of an octagonal wing on the south porch of Bingham Hill.

Four horses helped work the soil at Bingham Hill early in this century.

Dalton Parmly had over one hundred cows in 1914, selling his milk to Garfield Grover, the Lafayette Street dairy. According to a March 20, 1914 *Monmouth Press* account, Parmly had ordered a new milking machine powered by an electric motor that milked four cows at a time and sixty cows an hour. This photograph dates from *c.* 1914.

The wooded path is possibly Bingham Avenue, looking north from Parmly's. That vista could provide a view of the hills across the river, in the absence of present tree height. There were also extensive paths on the farm.

Dalton Parmly was fond of dogs and is shown here with two of them under one of the great trees of Bingham Hill. Parmly was an Elk, a Mason, and a long-time member of the Rumson Fire Department. He died in January 1938 and is buried at Rumson Cemetery. The property is famed for its trees, still possessing what is believed to be the oldest black walnut tree in Monmouth County.

Saint George's Episcopal Church was organized on July 7, 1874, with its edifice on the southeast corner of Ridge Road and Bellevue Avenue completed in the summer of 1875. The architect was A.J. Bloor of New York and the builder was Henry W. Wilson. It is important as an early, small, well-designed country church. Selecting a location was a critical issue in the sparsely settled summer community; the Sea Bright Bridge opened in 1870 and growth would follow near it. The church relocated to its present spot near the bridge and Shrewsbury River in 1908 (see p. 120) in order to service a larger community. (From *Seaside Souvenir*.)

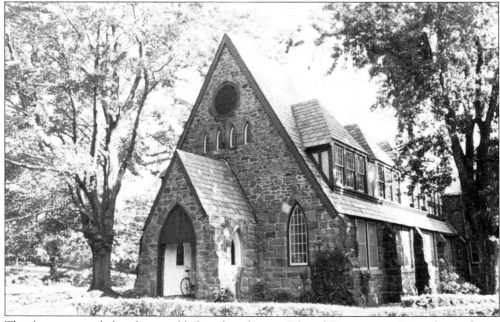

The deconsecrated church was added to the adjacent Edward Dean estate. Dean donated it to the Rumson Country Day School, which organized in 1926. Additions were built and a second-story interior constructed. The original structure is remarkably preserved, both in this 1974 view and today. The expanded dormers, built to increase room on the second story, are the only visible change. A major classroom building was attached at the rear, and is barely visible in this photograph.

This *c.* 1928 picture received a second chance for publication. Red Bank artist Evelyn Leavens (bottom left) indicated it could have appeared in *The First Fifty Years*, Edgar Blake's history of the Rumson Country Day School. However, she withheld it, not wanting to reveal her age then. Now? The world can know she was born September 25, 1924. (Send her a card.) Another student of note is Rosalind Wilson (middle row right), daughter of the writer and granddaughter of the lawyer, each named Edmund Wilson.

The Rumson Field Club baseball team seemed a contented crew in 1935. Perhaps they were enjoying a good season. The players are, from left to right: (front row) Floyd Roger, Jiggi Fowler (a good, old-style baseball nickname), Ed Junko, Sam Scalzo, Bert Emmons, and John Parmly; (back row) Ellsworth Soden, Charlie Elenberger, Bob Thorsen, Harold Thompson, Frank Young, and John Shea. The man in the suit is not identified.

Saint George's by-the-River Episcopal Church on Lincoln Avenue was erected in 1907–1908, designed by Walker & Gillette in the English Gothic style and built by Swallows and Howes, both firms from New York. The church was built as a simple cruciform with walls of granite and limestone. A major structural change was made in the 1950s. The south wall was removed for the construction of the chantry (a smaller place of worship beside the nave, at right in this picture) and The Chapel of the Resurrection (an enclosed room behind the chantry).

Saint George's was earlier located on Ridge Road (see p. 117), away from Rumson's center of population. Moving had been discussed for some while. William Everard Strong, a financier who held the unique distinction of having owned both a Rumson Road and a riverfront mansion, provided for a new church in his will. His widow Alice carried out his wishes, and the new Saint George's also became known as the Strong Memorial Church. (The Dorn's Collection.)

This aerial view of the Shrewsbury River shore south of the Sea Bright Bridge reflects change, including the expansion of Saint George's by-the-River. Note the additions to the original church, including the chantry to the right of the nave, and the series of halls and education buildings that obscure the view of the church from Lincoln Avenue. Rumson Road ends at the river, at the point where the bridge once crossed. The large building with the wing at an angle fronting Waterman Avenue (running the width of the picture) is the former Rumson Hotel. (Photograph by John Lentz.)

The Mary Owen Borden Memorial Carillon is installed in Saint George's tower. It was purchased by long-time warden Bertram Borden in England in 1934 and given to the church as a memorial to Borden's wife, who died the previous year. It was the first of his several generous gifts to Saint George's. The bells sound on Sunday mornings, during recitals, and on these dates significant to the Bordens: October 23 (Mary Owen's birth), September 24 (Mary Owen's death), and January 23 (the date of the Bordens' marriage).

The Rumson Hotel was located at 10 Waterman Avenue, overlooking the Shrewsbury River. It was moved there from Sea Bright in December 1914. This view dates from 1937, when Mary Hearnen Molloy bought it. The hotel was demolished in July 1984; three houses are on the site now.

Conover Park was founded in the 1880s by William W. Conover, Red Bank's most astute real estate investor of his time. It is outlined on the c. 1895 illustrated "bird's-eye view" map of Sea Bright, recently reproduced in George Moss' *Another Look*. It was renamed West Park after Conover divested. West Park in the post-World War II years was a well-spaced neighborhood of modest houses. High demand for waterfront property brought costlier projects and intensive development. This 1988 house designed by Paul Gugliotta at 98 Waterman Avenue takes full advantage of its 162-foot frontage on Oyster Bay.

Most land south of Rumson Road was left unbuilt during the town's early growth. Design challenges in the development of the southern shore included irregularly shaped property, which often prevented maximum exposure to the Shrewsbury River. Noboru Kobayashi's design for the Newton Liggett family in the late 1950s at 25 Heathcliff Road is placed well for river exposure, without resting on the edge of the bank. The one-story brick house with heavy beam and plank roof construction had a design element not common at the time, a skylight.

A chimney approximately 4 feet square is in the center of the main living area, surrounded by a skylight that allowed light to shine into the four rooms, which were separated by interior brick partitions as shown here. This view from the dining area shows half of the two-sided fireplace, which also opens to the family room opposite. Noboru Kobayashi, whose office is in Red Bank, is enjoying a long, successful career designing a variety of building types, including Middletown Township's public library and many of the area's most artistic houses.

J. Amory Haskell, who later built Oak Hill Farm in Middletown Township, arguably Monmouth County's finest country estate/gentleman's farm operation, began summer residency at the shore in Monmouth Beach c. 1895. This house was probably adjacent to the former Saint Peter's Church. It was moved to 59 South Shrewsbury Drive in Rumson. The house is in a fine state of preservation, although the porch has been removed. (From *Seaside Souvenir*.)

Congregation B'Nai Israel was founded in Red Bank in 1922, initially meeting in rented quarters, and later in a former house on Riverside Avenue. The congregation moved to Rumson in 1958 to this new synagogue at the southeast corner of Ridge and Hance Roads. It was designed by Kelly and Gruzen with a roof intended to appear as a tent; the concept was regarded as a novel and ingenious but the roof proved costly to build. A wing was added in 1971, about a decade after this photograph was taken.

The Oceanic Hook & Ladder Company receiving a new truck c. 1950. (The Dorn's Collection.)

The islands of the Navesink River are shown clearly, perhaps in the 1950s, tempting you to check the accuracy of your favorite map. Barley Point Island is at left, and the outlines of many houses are visible. Dorns Island is below it, close to the mainland. The strip at top is northern Sea Bright, while a few of the North Ward Avenue waterfront houses are barely visible at right. Black Point Horseshoe surrounds the pond at upper center. The Tredwell farmer's house is barely visible behind the small pond at center right. (The Dorn's Collection.)

John Hintelmann's store, which opened in 1896 at the juncture of Ridge Road and the Avenue of Two Rivers, had sufficient prominence to give the intersection the recognized name of Hintelmann's Corner. It was a trolley destination, as well as the post office. An earlier store was destroyed by fire on January 3, 1900. Robert D. Chandler designed this replacement, built that year. It, too, burned, in 1934. John died in 1917, with the business continued by his family. (Collection of John Rhody.)

A replacement store was designed by Myers and Shanley of Newark; the latter partner, Joseph J. Shanley, was a Rumsonian. Rumson contractor William Moncrieff & Company completed the building in a record twenty-one days. The wine and liquor area occupied the north, groceries the center, and meats the south. A hardware department sold kitchen utensils. The building was sold to the Oceanic Library Association in 1958. It opened as the remodeled library in 1959. This photograph was taken c. 1950s. (The Dorn's Collection.)

The borough lacked permanent offices for the first twenty years of its existence, and the council often met at the Center Street firehouse. In 1927, Mayor W. Warren Barbour gave the borough the grounds and Colonial Revival building, designed by Vance W. Forbert, that is the present borough hall on East River Road. The gift was made as a memorial to his parents, William and J. Adelaide Barbour. Warren was later a U.S. senator. Two Barbour homes can be seen on pp. 14 and 43. (Collection of Michael Steinhorn.)

These Oceanic Boy Scouts posed in the late 1910s for a photograph. T. Wilson, later a mayor of Rumson, was a member of this troop.

Red Bank artist Evelyn Leavens is shown here during her motorcycle days in the late 1940s on a Harley-Davidson with Warren Pomphrey at Oceanic. Although Evelyn also drove, she considered Warren's assistance in holding the heavy machine still at stop signs and traffic lights to be vital.

This is the end of a great trip. The means is the author's favorite mode of travel, the goat cart. This one was on the Borden estate c. 1917. Take another ride with Volume II and keep the pictures coming.